Selling – For Everyone

How to use your natural talents to maximise your sales potential

Selling – For Everyone
How to use your natural talents to maximise your sales potential

© Keith Place

ISBN: 978-1906316-68-6

All rights reserved.

Published in 2010 by HotHive Books, Evesham, UK.
www.thehothive.com

The right of Keith Place to be identified as the author of this work has been asserted by him in accordance with the Copyright, Designs and Patents Act 1988.

A CIP record of this book is available from the British Library.

No part of this publication may be reproduced in any form or by any means without prior permission from the author.

Printed in the UK by Latimer Trend, Plymouth

Contents

	Page
Introduction: what is selling?	5
1) Go prospecting and turn contacts into business	9
2) Making the right impression	15
3) An interlude: how to annoy your customers	23
4) Knowing what your customer needs	29
5) Persuasion and influencing	35
6) Telling everyone what your business does	41
7) Closing the sale and dealing with objection	47
8) Bringing it all together	53
About the author	55

Introduction: what is selling?

Introduction: what is selling?

If you own or work in a business, and if you have a product or service that you need to sell, then it's you I'm talking to. If you are a busy business owner and you feel that you need more from your people, then I'm talking to you too. If you're a salesperson and feel that you need to 'sharpen your axe', then I am sure you will pick up many useful tips.

That is why this book is called *Selling – For Everyone*.

We all sell in some way or another. Also, we all buy: this allows us to see selling from the other side of the table and is a valuable way of learning about what selling is and what it shouldn't be.

So, look around you and learn about selling from everyone in everyday situations.

> If we are all doing it, we must have an inherent ability both to buy and sell. This book puts some of these abilities in the spotlight and with the emphasis on selling, explains how your abilities can be used to make you and your business more successful.

What is selling?
It is described in many ways. Here are two of my interpretations:

- Selling is persuading someone to give you what you want in return for something you give to them.
- Selling is about enabling a transaction to take place after some sort of discussion or interaction with another person.

Other sources might focus on the fact that selling is a process, cycle or framework. Of course, we apply method and process to most areas of life, and indeed in business we need some structure and process, however, I will show you in this book that selling is more about the human things and less about processes. We won't shy away from process, but we will embrace the 'people skills' side.

> **Selling is about:**
> - Common understanding between people
> - Knowledge of each other and each other's business
> - Dialogue between different parties
> - Empathising with people
> - Building trust and mutual respect
> - Creating resonance, and so on.

The best salespeople I have come across demonstrate these traits and approaches and use them all the time when selling. The worst salespeople do not display these traits, and fall into a stereotype or category that gets selling a bad name.

> **Selling is not:**
> - Telling
> - Creating pressure
> - An argument that you can win
> - Just having a good product
> - Creating dissonance.

What skills do you need?

Listening is a key skill in selling, and believe it or not, we are going to spend time talking about how to listen! In addition,

Introduction: what is selling?

you will need to be able to think, plan, smile, talk and probably shake hands. If it sounds as if I'm being flippant, then you don't know how I feel about selling: I love it because I like getting to know people, their business, what I might be able to do for them and, ultimately, getting paid for what I love doing – which is helping them to be better at selling. So there is no flippancy here, but I do like to keep it simple and enjoyable, because it can be.

I begin this book in the firm belief that everyone can sell. Everyone can get more from their client meetings. Everyone can increase their confidence in front of clients. Selling really can be for everyone. I want you to use your natural talents to maximise your sales potential.

What needs to happen now is that you remove any preconceived ideas and concerns about selling or becoming a 'salesperson'. Let yourself absorb the idea that selling is all about people, relationships, understanding, values and needs. Unless we get these things right (luckily, they are inherent in all of us), we cannot use some of the other sales skills that are often less attractive but still very necessary and require a certain amount of process or discipline, such as opening, questioning, closing, objection handling and so on. (We will come on to those later.)

There is so much you can do to make sure that you are effective at selling, and much of it can be done before you even have a meeting or a telephone conversation about business.

1. Go prospecting and turn contacts into business

1. Go prospecting and turn contacts into business

Finding clients

Naturally, you will need to find people with whom you can do business or who may want your services. An important part of the sales process is prospecting. You have to search for gold before you can become rich, or before you can even stake a claim. You need to find where it is located, you usually have to dig, sift or pan for gold, and this requires time, effort and planning.

Prospecting for potential business leads is no different. You have to learn to look in the right places. You have to be persistent. It will require time and effort to accumulate a good number of potential business appointments, and you will need a plan so that you look for prospects in an organised way.

Finding clients plan

| Who are they? | What do they do? | Where are they? | Why do they need what I have? |

You could do worse than approach the problem as above. The 'who' is merely identifying with whom you would like to do business. You can be as specific as you like with any of these points – in fact, it will make your search easier if you can focus in on some of your potential targets rather than generalise too much. The 'what' can give you focus on a particular type of business or person. The 'where' can relate to geography, ie UK or Denver, Colorado, etc, but it also can mean where they can be found, which journals they will read, which industry bodies they are aligned with, etc. The 'why' is making sure that you have considered their needs and that you are making this about them, not about you.

It's about what they can get out of you – not what you can get out of them!

Where can you start?

As you begin to use your 'finding clients' plan, you can look close by: begin with all the people you know – friends, family, previous work colleagues and current clients. Include people you meet at your sports club, down the pub, at quiz nights. However, what do you say to these people? Well, what do you normally do when you meet people? Talk to them. Be interested in them. Ask about them. Get to know them better, whether you think you know them or not. You will get the chance to let them know about you, don't rush it. Make sure you allow people the time to ask about you. Start working on the list mentioned previously: build some common understanding, knowledge, dialogue. Selling isn't telling!

When you're talking to people, don't push your product down their throat. Let the conversation occur naturally. It's amazing how quickly people will ask you about your business if you let them – and here is the real gem:

> If they like you and trust you, they will remember you and refer you to others.

1. Go prospecting and turn contacts into business

As you will have gathered by now, my approach suggests that selling is as much about your networks as it is about looking in specific places for specific people. Build your network of contacts through social media such as Twitter, Facebook, LinkedIn or any of the many online networks out there, whichever one of these, or a combination of them, works for you. Find places locally where you can attend organised networking events. There will be several in your area. Read local papers, see who is doing what and open your mind to opportunity. They are a great way to get business appointments, but the rule about not pushing it still exists here.

Of course, networking is about business and not just widening your social circle (although the two are more related than you may realise). Therefore, you should focus on the type of people and businesses with whom you would like to make contact. Think about where they spend their time, what they read, which associations they will be part of and so on. Now you can begin to apply your plan, working towards creating a list of people and how you might like to contact them.

Many people try to play the 'numbers game'. They collect contacts both online and through local meeting groups and expect business to follow. Of course, they might get some business if they have a sensible offer but if they narrow their search and speak to more people who really need what they have to offer, then a greater degree of success will follow.

So, look in the right places for the people best suited to take value from what you offer – then give them a chance to like you. There is a lot of free activity that you can use to market your business and get yourself noticed. In my experience, meeting people is by far the most powerful, rewarding and enjoyable. Once you have found them, or they have found you, what next?

> **Get organised – have a plan** ◄ ● ● ● ● ●
> Know who you want to find, and look where they are likely to be.

1. Go prospecting and turn contacts into business

2. Making the right impression

2. Making the right impression

So, you have found people to talk to about business, and now you want to create an environment where sales can take place.

Think first about the impression you want people to have of you. Your overall behaviour, dress, voice, language, body language, handshake, facial expression and so on, will all affect the way that people perceive you, and will create a lasting and convincing impression. Remember, as I hinted in the last chapter, you want to give people the chance to like but also to respect and admire you. People generally buy from people they like, respect and admire. As Aristotle said:

> *"To be convincing, you need to learn how to win over minds with logic, to win over hearts with emotion and to manage yourself so that you can be seen as authoritative."*

First impressions

First impressions are strange things. For example, I met a young and enthusiastic salesperson on a course in the 1990s.

He arrived on the first day of the sales course in a shiny silvery-grey suit, black shoes with tassles and white socks. He wore at least two gold rings on each hand, one of which was a sovereign ring, a gold chain around his neck and a gold bracelet. When he greeted us, he said 'Awright? 'Ow's it 'anging!' I kid you not, these were his first words to me. If I had the ability, James Bond style, to raise one eyebrow, it would have been at that moment.

2. Making the right impression

He created a certain impression on me and my fellow coursemates, and in reading this you already will have created an impression of him too. At the end of the course he was conscious of the impression that he gave and moderated his style a little.

Why should he moderate his style? Well, to be honest, it's up to you how you dress, speak and act. However, the impression you give will stay with people. All I ask is that you are conscious of it.

This guy was in fact a really great bloke and very good salesperson – why shouldn't he be? He was friendly, loved to ask questions, he told really funny stories and was nice to be around. He didn't lose any of that, but he did learn that certain types of language and greetings may put people off. In his role as a salesperson his customers may expect a little less fashion and a little more formality.

On the second day of the course he came down to breakfast in the same suit, wearing just one ring, black socks and looking like the professional salesperson he was training to become, rather than a spiv.

I agree with the phrase 'You only have one chance to create a first impression', but often you can have the chance to recreate or remould the impression that people have of you. Be yourself, first and foremost. Moderate the extremes that might make people uncomfortable. Enhance the qualities that people may be looking for.

2. Making the right impression

Give people the chance to like you ◄ ● ● ● ● ●
Enhance the qualities people may be looking for.
Be yourself – first and foremost.

Engaging people ◄ ● ● ● ● ● ● ● ● ● ●

Now, think about how you engage people in conversation. Start a dialogue with a question. Often, the best way to get the dialogue going is to ask open questions, those requiring more than a 'yes' or 'no' answer. Get to know the person and show genuine interest in them. This is rapport-building and helps to build trust. If you and I were to meet and all you did was talk about yourself and how good you are, I would politely extricate myself from the conversation and go and find someone more interesting. What makes someone interesting? They allow the natural see-saw and flow of conversation to occur. They tell stories, ask questions, show empathy and argue – all of these things. We are far more likely to build rapport with, and therefore learn to trust, a person with a more rounded approach to conversing than someone who is driven to talk at us.

You may have heard of the 'elevator pitch'. This is the approach that some 'experts' will say is indispensible for your business and something you need to have prepared for when you meet someone in a lift. (Let's face it: most of us do not spend a lot of time in lifts. We do not necessarily speak to people there and we certainly do not sell to people in them). There is a part of my profession that seems to think that unless we force an opportunity to occur, we will miss out on talking to a chief executive who is standing next to us in a queue. If we pitch at them, they will immediately be engaged with what we are saying and hire us on the basis of some kind of clever sales pitch taking place in a public environment. This will not and does not happen (I think it was supposed to happen in the 1980s but I never witnessed it – except in Hollywood movies). It will not happen to you either if all you have to say is some kind of sales pitch. Let me explain.

There is an accepted code for organised networking meetings where it is possible to explain a little about who you are and what you do in under a minute. That's fine: it is an organised and accepted way of making introductions. However, even at these organised meetings, many people get this wrong by being too fearful that their message needs to say everything about them and their business during that minute. They just try to cram in more words, and this does not work. I have talked about having an elevator pitch in some of my sales seminars. I do not mind the tag, but it's best to avoid the traps.

My simple advice here is to make people like you in that time. They are more likely to remember you and therefore will want to know more about you. Avoid rattling off a list of things that you and your business does, which is boring. Don't push your services into people's faces. Let them get to know you. Better still, get to know them first. Get to like them for who they are and get them to like you in return. It is far more effective. Get your introduction down to a greeting and a smile and then ask a question. You have said enough already for now.

2. Making the right impression

> People will not remember you for your lists. Saying too many things communicates too little.

If you are talking to a group, ask a general rhetorical question such as: 'How many people in the room would like to talk to a good listener about their business and what they are looking for?' If you're speaking to an individual, why not just say, 'Hello, good to meet you. My name is …' Then let them speak. Let them tell you a little about them. Encourage them with more gentle questions. See, selling is not that hard. If you are asked what you do then, of course, have an answer locked away that will give a little about you, your business and why you are different, without listing your full range of services and life history.

Another way to engage people, and be more memorable for the right reasons, is to use stories. Stories and anecdotes are a great way of swapping information, ideas and getting to know and like people. It is not appropriate to walk up to a stranger and tell them a story, but you can illustrate conversations with anecdotes and stories far more effectively than by descriptions. Why? Because stories are about people, not things. Stories are about how people interact with the world. Therefore, your customers can relate to stories and often can join in with stories of their own.

Good marketers use stories all the time to show you how a product or service can fit in with your business or life. They would need to spend hours and hours trying to describe the same thing.

2. Making the right impression

Being memorable

You will probably have heard the phrase 'People buy from people' – but if you hadn't, you have now. It's true. People buy from people that they like, trust, respect and remember. I have never heard someone say that they are going to get their printing from 'The guy I met last week, you know, whatshisname? The sort of average bloke who went on and on about himself'. They are much more likely to say: 'I met a guy last week, Steve, from a local printers – nice guy, supports Oxford United, takes his little lad there most Saturdays. I took his card.'

Steve obviously made the right impression by being personable, knowledgeable and memorable and, judging by what was said about him, he clearly had a conversation where personal information was exchanged. He allowed people to get to like him. He probably told stories about the football matches he had been to with his son.

Being memorable isn't always natural behaviour for most of us. Some people have natural charisma and some have to work harder at it, but you can be remembered for many good things, and they are not all about big personality.

> Create the right impression by sharing personal and business information and sharing stories instead of descriptions.

You will remember people for all kinds of reasons. They might:
- Have been really helpful
- Have a really nice smile

2. Making the right impression

- Make people laugh
- Be polite and kind
- Be full of fun
- Be genuinely interested in you
- Have hobbies or interests that coincide with yours
- Have been very knowledgeable about a topic that interests you
- Just own a cat and you like cats
- Even have a business offer that interests you.

If you have taken the time to create a positive lasting impression and have shown a genuine interest in the people you meet, you are on the road to selling. Without this first level of trust, understanding and common ground, it is very unlikely that you will create business opportunities from the meeting.

> Be genuinely interested in the people you meet to create trust and understanding.

Can you create the right impression on the phone? You know that the answer is 'yes' and all the same rules apply – but without the visual, you need to create that. You do this with your voice, diction, dialogue and personality. You can still create interest by listening and being interested in the answers, and by telling stories.

The different media we use to communicate have very similar rules. Apply these as universally as you can and you are creating the environment where sales are taking place, without even knowing it.

3. An interlude: how to annoy your customers

3. An interlude: how to annoy your customers

I received a call very recently. I feel the need to tell you about it, because it is a fantastic lesson in how not to sell to anyone – ever.

A salesperson called me, and his endgame was to sign me up for an alternative supply for my business telephone and internet connections. I am always ready to listen to salespeople, notwithstanding my interests in sales, because there may be some benefit for me and my business and because people deserve a chance.

I think his script said: 'Engage the customer in an argument and do not listen to anything they say.' He began by trying to establish that I was in fact the person he had just called. I said I was, but he was adamant that I should prove myself. I explained that I knew perfectly well who I was and that as he had just called me, he might want to take my word for it.

Clearly thrown by this immediate irrelevance, he started telling me that his records showed that I was paying the maximum tariff for my calls and that he could save me money. This, apparently, was a statement of fact. He then asked who my supplier was. Surely, he already knew that or he wouldn't know about my tariff, would he? When I pointed that out, he just asked again who my supplier was. I told him.

He then proceeded to tell me that he would save me money, change my line, send me one bill and all I needed to do was transfer some money to his company immediately to start the process. This one-way 'conversation' was all finished with the phrase 'Yeah?', spoken as a question. Fantastic: in just a few minutes he knew all about me, my supplier, my rates, my business requirements, my personal circumstances, my ability to pay – and all without asking any pertinent questions. A sales genius!

At this point I continued to encourage the call for the sport of it, as I had decided in the first few moments that I was not buying anything he could possibly try and sell to me. I pushed back a little, as one might expect, and thought up a few obstacles for him to clamber over: I am tied to an agreement; I am happy with my current supplier; I am wary of change and share the costs across two businesses. His response, 'So, you don't want to save any money then?', leaped all obstacles in one gigantic bound.

I could not carry on the deception any longer, and explained that I would not be changing my supplier in his favour and that he needn't call again. He hung up abruptly and that, you would think, would be an end to the whole sorry saga – but no, it gets better.

His colleague called back several hours later (he might have been a supervisor) to ask why I was not taking up the offer, and did I not realise that I could save my business some money? Intrigued, I asked how they were going to overcome my concerns.

3. An interlude: how to annoy your customers

Now, at this point you would expect one of two answers. I was either expecting him to say 'What concerns?', or an attempt to overcome some or all of them. He surpassed my wildest expectations. I was totally in awe of the answer. He said, 'Send me a copy of a bill. Do you have a fax? We can save you money. Don't you realise that you should be cutting your costs, you know, the economy and all that – yeah?'

Not only are my concerns rendered totally invalid due to all the money he is about to save me, but I am a very stupid businessperson who should realise that cutting costs might be a good thing right now, for some reason to do with the economy, or something. Brilliant.

I cut the call at this point and explained again that there was no need or desire for me to change, and that there was no need for me to receive any calls from their company again.

Luckily for all of us, there have been no further calls.

> If a person, whether buying or selling, feels in any way uncertain that a transaction should take place, it shouldn't until you have been able to determine how to remove that uncertainty completely.

Sadly, this approach is more common than it should be. If there is no listening, empathy, common understanding or dialogue, it is merely telling. More unfortunate still, some people will have been bullied by this type of approach at some time.

Let us see this for what it was: an attempt to make a transaction with no concern for meeting the need of a customer and certainly no requirement to add value or develop a relationship based on trust.

So, what should you do? It is simple. Ask appropriate questions.

- Be genuinely interested in the answers
- Seek clarification if you need to understand something more fully
- Let the person at the other end of the phone hear that you are also a person
- Don't push too hard.

However, do not think that being persuasive is always being pushy. Persuasion is a key skill in selling, but there are ways to ask. You can ask with a smile in your voice. Ask politely. It doesn't hurt and will always get better results than if you are pushy or aggressive.

4. Knowing what your customer needs

4. Knowing what your customer needs

The only way to know what anybody needs is by asking questions: good questions. What is a good question? One that elicits a response – quite easy, really. However, so many people are not good at this: they ask too few questions and bolt to the end of their own sales journey before it has really begun. In fact, they are on a sales journey all by themselves – everyone else has disembarked.

Here is a process map which will help you to understand where you are during this journey.

Where to start?

If you've referred to Chapter 2 on creating the right impression, then the ball is already rolling. You will have taken steps to be liked and get to know the person with whom you might like to do business.

Now you have a sense of rapport, you can begin to ask more searching questions about their work, business, role and so on. Take small steps and remember, be interested and curious about the responses. Don't just rush to the next question without considering the responses and demonstrating that you have heard the answer and are interested.

Can you plan what you would like to ask? Of course you can. First, you need to ask yourself two questions: 'What do you need to know?' and 'What would you like to know?' Once these are in your mind (or better still, on paper), you can think about the type of questions to ask that will take you along the path towards the answers. Some people write down specific questions; I write down what I need to know and then make up the questions as I go. Find a way that suits your style and go with it. A modest amount of planning will help you to remain in control of your own pace, will stop you missing things and from jumping ahead, as mentioned earlier.

Once you have thought about what you want to know and you have posed the question to the client, concentrate hard on the answers. During a cold call on the telephone, how many people ask 'How are you?' when they call you? They don't wait for an answer, they are just filling in time to get to a sales pitch. This is no way to build rapport. I don't have a problem with the question as such, but don't ask it if you don't care about the answer.

If you ask a better question such as 'How long have you been at Smith and Johnson?', wait for the reply and perhaps make a comment that follows on: 'Oh, not a long time then. What kind of things have you been working on these last few months?' As you can see, the questions can start to link together. This shows that you are listening and are interested in the answers.

> Be interested in what your customer is saying. Link your questions to show that you are listening. Use 'confirming' questions to show you have listened and understood. Avoid merely repeating the question back – you are not a parrot.

Have a point ◄ ● ● ● ● ● ● ● ● ● ● ●

It can look pretty bad for you if the conversation drifts around aimlessly and you leave a meeting with reams of notes but no apparent conclusions. Let the customer know why a conversation is a good idea. You could say:

> *"It's a great opportunity to find out more about your role in Smith and Johnson and to understand if we can be of help to each other. I'm interested to know more about what you do here."*

Let the person know the kind of approach you would like to take. Ask whether they mind if you take notes. I was at several meetings where notes could not leave the room because we were discussing pricing and strategy, so I am glad I asked. Some topics are confidential or sensitive – this does not happen often, but it is good to ask.

Asking good questions and listening to the answers is the major part of getting to know your potential customer better. It is also about getting to like and know your customer. Questioning is the 'foreplay' in sales. Without it, your potential partner could be left cold!

Value: what is it? ◄ ● ● ● ● ● ● ● ●

Part of understanding customer needs means that you should have a grasp of how they see the value in the products and services that they buy. You have to know where the customer places value. Let me explain.

Some people want to know what a product is, and the price. Some may want to know a little more about what a product does. Others go a bit further and need to see a return on their purchase. It could be that a product or service will take costs out of their business, or make them more money, or save them time, and so on.

Then there are those who look further ahead and wonder how your product or service will improve their business or lives into the future. They may want to know that you can make their business stronger, faster or more sustainable, but they are certainly looking further ahead.

Imagine how and why you buy certain products and services, then apply that to the examples above. It helps to understand your own perspectives.

> Find your customers' perspectives and find the value in your offer to match.

You now know much more about what your customer needs, and can help them to see the true value in your product or service.

5. Persuasion and influencing

5. Persuasion and influencing

Chapter 2 dealt with how you might create the right impression, and this chapter will deal with the skills and behaviour that you can work on with regard to influencing the people around you from the very beginning of your relationship. Getting people to like and trust you is always the place to start.

How do people view you?

Within the first few minutes, people will have a fully formed impression of you. Some of these were covered in Chapter 2, but what affects the way that people see you? There are many factors, including:

- Attractiveness
- Gender
- Sexuality
- Age
- Voice
- Ethnicity
- Physique
- Social status
- Education
- Cultural background
- Place or country of residence, and much more.

The people you meet will form their impressions based on all of these things before they have listened to what you say. If you want to influence the way people form their impression of you, it is necessary to draw their attention in the right direction in the first few seconds.

Making an impact will draw their attention, begin to influence their opinion of you and what you have to say, and keep you in their memory.

So, create impact and be remembered. The behaviours below will create impact. Being aware of these impactful behaviours can make you even more compelling and persuasive. For example, think of someone in the public eye and ask yourself why they make an impact on you. How many of these traits do they display? Are they:

- Powerful
- Passionate
- Inspirational
- Charismatic
- Tenacious
- Altruistic
- Honest
- Uncompromising
- Personable
- Engaging, Or
- Something Else?

They are likely to be all of these things and a few others besides. They will certainly have a mix of these things in their make-up – and, by the way, so do you. However, people will have a 'driving behaviour'. This is a trait which rises to the surface above all others. It is good to have an appreciation of your driving behaviour, while finding your blend of different behaviours and being able to adjust the recipe where necessary.

5. Persuasion and influencing

Driving behaviour

Let's think about that last statement. If you are in a social setting with close friends, your language, tone of voice, diction, body language and overall behaviour will be different from when you are in a first meeting with your partner's family, business colleagues or a potential client. You have the innate ability to change your 'behaviour recipe' to suit any given situation. However, you will still have a driver – that strongest element of your behaviour for which you are known and loved.

Bearing that in mind, what is your driving behaviour? What is your strongest trait and does it reflect well on you in any given circumstance? You can use the table below to help identify different types of behaviour and which of these you display most and least. If you don't think they apply to you, don't mark it. Be honest with yourself and identify your strongest driver(s). Use the third column to write down your thoughts as you go through the exercise.

DRIVING BEHAVIOURS		
DRIVER	RANK 1-5	DETAILS
POWERFUL		
PASSIONATE		
INSPIRATIONAL		
CHARISMATIC		
TENACIOUS		
ALTRUISTIC		
HONEST		
UNCOMPROMISING		
PERSONABLE		
ENGAGING		

Having understood your driving behaviour, it is now important to understand what attitudes are important in influencing. You will need to adopt an attitude that allows your influence to develop. These are skills that we all possess, but as with your driving behaviour, it is good to understand which of these are strong within you and which need work. You should give yourself a grade against all of these, and again, use the third column to note down your thoughts as you go.

INFLUENCING ATTITUDES		
ATTITUDES	RANK 1-5	DETAILS
FLEXIBILITY		
PATIENCE		
TRUST		
CONFIDENCE		
CREDIBILITY		
OPENNESS		
CONSISTENCY		
COURAGE		
SELF-KNOWLEDGE		
ENTHUSIASM		

Understanding influencing attitudes ◀ ● ● ● ●

Can you be flexible as well as consistent? Are you able to demonstrate enthusiasm and be patient? These are complex interpersonal skills, and we all use them to different degrees in our personal and professional lives. We certainly all have them. Understanding when to adopt certain attitudes can be very powerful in how we influence others. It is about finding the right blend, when to be persistent and when to give a little; when to be enthusiastic or when to be patient and allow room for a prospect to make their own decision.

5. Persuasion and influencing

Once you understand your personal driving behaviour and your own blend of influencing attitudes you can begin to see yourself in the way that others see you. This is empowering. Once you start to feel comfortable with these concepts, you can learn to modify your behaviour without changing who you are. This allows people to form new and different impressions of you. You are now starting to create the influence around you that will improve your abilities to sell – and it was all about people skills.

> Find a blend of traits and behaviours to suit a situation or a particular customer and display them. They are all you. All you are doing is applying the right behaviour at the right time.

6. Telling everyone what your business does

6. Telling everyone what your business does

Incredibly, this is a lot harder for most businesses to answer than they would admit to, but it is important for you to get this right. You should have a good idea of what it is that you do, why you do it, who you would like to do it for, and so on. The impressions that other people will have of you and your business (and this is particularly relevant if you are selling a service), are often different from your own.

Once people know what you do, you can begin to show people why they should choose you instead of anyone else.

Positioning

The skill used here is called 'positioning', of which there are two parts:

1. Having a position
2. Positioning your offer.

The first part, having a position, is what the world sees when it looks at your business. Your business needs to have a point. Why does your business exist? What does it offer, to whom and why?

Eventually, together with other messages, this will become your brand. Branding is all about your identity. A part of that identity is your logo and the visual impact of your business, but there is much more to it than that. How other people understand or perceive what you do is your position.

> Things a position must be: clear, simple, straightforward, different, real and true.

With Chapter 2 in mind, think about the impression that you would like your business to create. What perception would you like people to have of your business?

- What about the size – do you want to appear small or large?
- What is the scope of your activities?
- What type of customers would you like to work with?
- What are the values of your business?
- What way would you like to treat people, and to be treated?

This is your position. You have defined it to make the right impression on your potential market place, based on your best possible understanding.

> The position of your business is what you tell people that you are, and what you tell people about what it is you do.
>
> It is matching your business to the needs of your potential market.

The second part is actual positioning (the part most commonly referred to). It is the skill required to mould your offer to suit the customer's or prospect's ways of looking at things.

6. Telling everyone what your business does

During dialogue you will get an impression of what the customer is looking for – you will pick up signals. In addition, you will get an idea of where they place value. This is your opportunity to position your offer to match your prospect's needs (as we discussed in Chapter 4, Knowing what your customer needs).

Here is an example. Imagine a scenario where you are about to sell your old car. It is a small, economical, clean and tidy car, but you need something bigger.

A young couple come to view your car. You find out by talking to them for a few minutes that they are renting their first apartment together, they have recently finished university and now they need a car for visiting relatives.

It is safe to assume that the value they will place on the car will be partly based on low running costs and reliability. So initially, you could position yourself in that camp. Do that by telling them a little bit about the economical motoring you have enjoyed from this car (a story). This is a safe position.

Virtually no one would want a car to be uneconomical anyway, but to them, economy is likely to have high value. Then ask a few more questions. It may transpire that they want a little car they can love. It will be their first car together.

Position yourself as someone who is sad to lose your beloved car (tell another story about how the car has taken you to some lovely picnics and open air concerts) but alas, you need something larger and you only want it to go to a good home.

Now, imagine that the potential customer is a young man, 18 years old, and obviously into fashion and music (you could hear his mp3 player halfway down the street). A good starting position might be that the car is all in original condition and has been easy to work on, then ask some more questions.

It may turn out that he is looking for economy too and a low insurance premium. He may also want to 'pimp' it up a bit. So, you position the car as a wolf in sheep's clothing. Small and economical, but easy to modify and retune for better performance and a new look. It has retro qualities. This guy is not going to buy on the premise that he is giving it a loving home – he might want to strip it down, respray it and screw lots of new bits to its bodywork.

Eitherway, the car can be sold to either of these people and anyone else too. How would you sell the same car to an old couple, a single mum, a teacher? There will be a position to suit these buyers, and yet it remains the same product. Think about your products or services in exactly the same way.

6. Telling everyone what your business does

Not everyone will see or value the same products, attributes or features of the products in the same way. Your ability to position your productor service to suit the way that people value your offer can be a very powerful tool in your armoury.

> Positioning is matching your product or service to fit the specific needs of a potential buyer. It is not pretending that the product or service is something it is not!

7. Closing the sale and dealing with objection

Closing the sale

Closing is about gaining some form of commitment from the person looking to buy your product or service. It does not have to be taking their money from them right now. Closing, or asking for the next step, is an expected part of the sale and will not shock or annoy the prospect or customer, unless they are not ready to go there. (Therefore, if you haven't read Chapter 6 on positioning, it might be a good idea to do this first.)

If you position correctly, at the right time and for all the right reasons, you will get very few objections at this stage. Let's recap briefly.

> You have spent time and genuine energy on getting to know your prospect, understanding their needs and letting them get to know and like you for who you are.
>
> They respect you for what you know, and they trust and like you as a person and someone with whom they can do business.
>
> You have skilfully shown that you are an open and understanding business partner and have been able to resonate with them all through the growing relationship.
>
> After some good dialogue, you have positioned your offer based on the information that they have given you. You understand where they place value and can deliver the right solution to them.
>
> In other words, you have matched your offer to meet their needs. Their needs have been central to your conversations and you have shown empathy for their situation.

Now, you should suggest the next steps. This is the close. Make a proposal based on taking some action. How can you do that?

1. Very briefly summarise where you are now: 'So, from all you have said, it sounds as if Smith and Johnson could really benefit from an uplift in sales performance.'
2. Briefly summarise your position: 'As we talked about, Oxford Sales Consultants can offer the help and advice which will enable you to move towards this sales performance improvement you are looking for.'
3. Suggest the next steps: 'I will draw up an improvement plan with costs and timescales. Let's meet to discuss the details next week.'
4. Thank them: 'Thanks for the meetings that have led up to this. I'm looking forward to getting this project going with you.'

There is nothing pushy about this if all the other steps are in place. However, we can see that this might be pushy if we have just jumped straight into this phase of the dialogue. If we miss out the chat, rapport, influencing, knowledge-gathering, positioning and summarising, we will get objections. Nonetheless, we will still get some objections earlier in the sales dialogue.

Dealing with objections

I am not going to teach you how to overcome every objection that can be thrown at you. Why not? Because if the objection is real and deep-rooted enough, and you try too hard, the buyer will not like you or trust you. They will feel pressured. Ask yourself whether you like to be pressured. No? Well, the buyer will not like it either.

Most people do not respond well to being pressured by others into doing something before they are ready. They may never be ready. You are not their only option in life, so don't take on that mantle; all you are trying to do is get to the heart of an objection to see if you can overcome it. If you do, then you may help the customer to make a decision.

What will always make the decision easy? Annoying the customer by leaping to the wrong answers before you have asked good questions and really understood the objection.

What kind of objections might we encounter? There are four types.

1. Needing more
These are people who ask for more information, more time or more guidance from others in their organisation, etc.

After you have helped by allowing more time and providing more information – and, by the way, many people need to see and hear more information before they are ready to make a commitment to a new supplier – you can push a little. You can say:

> *Is there anything else you need to help you to make a decision on this?*

If you would like to move this on, is there anyone else you would like me to talk to?

Are there any gaps you can see in my proposal that we can work on?

2. Fear of change

This is not exactly fear, but resistance to change. I am like this, so if a seller tries to railroad me into a decision which they feel is a foregone conclusion, I tend to push them away. If they are not skilled enough to ask some simple questions about what more I need to help me reach a final decision, they are doomed. Let's examine this a little more closely. What is it I am afraid of? I might have an existing relationship with a current supplier and feel a sense of loyalty. I might see change as more workload, or it might just be an inconvenience. I might not like the unknown, preferring the familiar.

So, if I am asked gently what my concerns might be, I might share some of this information with them (if they are courteous, patient and professional). If I respond that I would consider another supplier as long as I am not required to do anything to make it happen and that I do not want to suffer any inconvenience as a result, the seller has more information to reassure me. They can now explain what the change will require in terms of input from me and what the change will look like. If this is done to my satisfaction and I now feel comfortable, I can make a decision. It might still be negative, but the seller has done all they can. That is all any of us can do.

3. Loyalty to someone else

I can understand this, and I would not change unless my relationship was not as strong as I thought. What I would ask as the seller is whether or not there was a chance to discuss change or just to keep in touch. Why apply pressure when we are agreed that relationships are key to business? All you can do here is demonstrate your credibility through testimonials and referrals and then leave the buyer to ponder just how strong their current relationship is. Keep the lines of communication open and respect other people's relationships.

4. Price, cost and value

Let's face it: we have all resisted buying because the price felt too high. Was it too high? Sometimes, yes. When we compare like for like and one price is higher, we will often buy the cheapest. Sometimes we do not understand the value. We do not know why a particular product or service adds any value to us. This is not about price. It is about a mismatch between what we think we need and what we are being offered.

Occasionally, the price objection is a very real concern that the capital outlay is too much at that time. A small business may want what you have, but funds are not available to buy. Will more persuasion change this? No. Will asking more questions about timing, payment plans, staged payments or payment on results, etc help? Yes, it might.

There are many forms of objection. The key to overcoming them is to understand them more fully. Only then can you actually reposition to any effect.

8. Bringing it all together

8. Bringing it all together

Understand what selling means and get your natural abilities, thoughts and attitude to selling in line.

Find people to talk to and keep finding more of the right people.

Learn what impression you make on people and how to modify your inherent traits to suit all occasions.

Ask questions. Be curious. Get to know about people and their businesses. Find out what they really need, what they value and if you are able to deliver it.

Learn how to use your natural talents to persuade and influence the people you meet, your current customers and clients. Develop your skills and be aware of the power of influencing.

Get to grips with positioning. First, have a clear position for your business. Second, learn how to be flexible with positioning according to your clients' needs. Remember, the same product or service looks different to different people.

Reposition accordingly.

Position and clarify. Check. Summarise. Then close by suggesting the next steps. You will get very few objections if you do this well. When you do get objections, try and understand the root cause – it's rarely the insurmountable issue that it appears to be.

Most of all, enjoy your interaction with people. Enjoy the time you can spend getting to know more people. Be interested and curious. Have great dialogue. Get you and your business out there among people.

This is selling – for everyone. Enjoy.

About the author

About The Author

Keith Place is the founder and director of Oxford Sales Consultants, which he established at the beginning of 2009. He has more than 20 years' experience in sales and marketing, much of which was spent in senior managerial level roles.

His experience, which he carries forward into his business, covers areas such as sales and sales management, marketing, marketing management and strategic planning, training, coaching and mentoring, key account management and planning, running strategic improvement programmes and change management.

Keith lives in Oxfordshire with his wife and family, enjoying the rural sporting and social life. He enjoys village cricket, coaching rugby, walking and training his Springer spaniel, reading and writing.